How to Succeed in Real Estate

How to Succeed in Real Estate

in Real Estate

A Step-By-Step Guide to Starting a Career as a Realtor

MORGAN A. MANOS

ISBN: 0692379339
ISBN 13: 9780692379332
Library of Congress Control Number: 2015901818
Morgan Manos, San Mateo, CA

Dedicated to everyone who has the drive to succeed.

Table of Contents

Introduction

I can't tell you how many times I've been at a mixer or mothers' club meeting or yoga class and had someone say to me, "How do you like the real estate business? I've always wanted to get into it!" Deciding to start a career in real estate is deciding to head down an exciting path. But while most envision the paycheck, not many know how to reach the top, let alone their first paycheck. Being a successful realtor takes much more than being a people person or having a love for architecture and interior design. I'm here to give you detailed, expert steps to transforming your newfound career choice into a career success.

Before I dive into how to succeed in the real estate business, let me tell you a little about myself. My name is Morgan Manos, and I am twenty-eight years old. I am a California realtor based in the San

Francisco Bay Area. I left the insurance sales world in 2012 to pursue a career in real estate. I joined my business partner as his marketing coordinator and spent the next year learning the business inside and out, observing top producers, and soaking up experience. I studied my butt off and aced the state exam the following summer. Applying the successful tactics that other top producers were employing, I quickly helped grow our business to rank among the state's top 2 percent of producers for 2013 and 2014.

If our business can succeed beyond all our expectations here, in one of the most expensive and competitive areas in the country, then this book can definitely help you succeed, no matter what part of the country you live in.

One

Passing the Test

There are two types of real estate licenses that you can obtain: The Brokers license, and the Sales Agent license. This book is geared towards someone who has decided they want to pursue a career as a real estate agent. What's the difference you ask? In a nutshell, people usually start off as sales agents before deciding they want to branch off to become a broker. A broker is the umbrella company in which you can conduct business. If you would like to operate as a broker, you likely own your own real estate agency and have experience with all avenues of the business. The agent works under the broker to conduct business as a representative of that brokerage.

I've taken two state exams in my life—the California State Insurance Broker's Exam and the California State Real Estate Agent's Exam—both of which I passed on the first try. Both were very similarly formatted and I applied the same study tactics to both: memorizing the practice exams and practicing over, and over. Kaplan is one option that offers both in class training as well as a self-study online course. I chose the online option for both my insurance and real estate sales agent exam. I found Kaplan to be sufficient and comprehensive in their exam-prep. Kaplan isn't the only online self-study course you can take; there are plenty that offer in-class programs as well. The self-study courses can be practiced at your own pace while the in class option requires physically attending an 8-hour day course for 5 or 6 days. I studied for my real estate sales agent exam while working full time as a real estate marketing coordinator, which gave me a perfect opportunity to apply concepts and learn vocabulary. All students have their own study pace and habits, but I highly recommend paying extra-close attention to the practice tests.

TESTING TIP: Memorize the practice exams and do them as many times as possible until you are getting 100 percent of the questions right. The

questions will be similar or identical to the ones on the California state exam.

While each state has its own preexamination requirements to adhere to, here are links to some online real estate exam-prep courses that are accepted in most states:

- http://www.kapre.com/real-estate-courses/
- http://www.reschool.com
- http://www.easy2pass.com

For additional resources and information on starting a career in real estate, local and state-level resources, as well as state-by-state requirements, visit the National Association of Realtors at http://www.realtor.org.

Finding a Mentor

The advice in this book is enough to provide you with a solid road map for success; however, it's a good idea to partner with a mentor early on in your career. There is something invaluable about pairing up with an experienced real estate producer. (Just to clarify the term, a *producer* in real estate is someone who produces business.) Some of the best tips and information I have picked up have come from listening to my mentor interact with buyers, sellers, lenders, other agents, and title company reps. Learning firsthand from an experienced mentor is the most efficient way to success.

TIP: If you want to be successful, do what successful people do. Pair up with a top producer as a marketing coordinator and assistant for six months. Most likely, you'll make about fifteen dollars an hour and have the opportunity to learn the day-to-day grind.

I would first check out craigslist or other job websites for any local realtors that may be looking for an assistant or marketing coordinator. Chances are if they have enough business being conducted to warrant hiring the help, they are likely successful in their trade. The quickest way to being hired as a real estate assistant or marketing coordinator is show eagerness to learn and an interest in becoming an agent. Make it known that you are not only looking to fill the open position but also looking for a long-term mentor. (Stroke the ego a little here! It works every time)

What can you gain from a mentor you ask? Aside from some sort of a paycheck while you muddle your way through the learning process, you will gain first hand experience dealing with both "business-as-usual" transactions as well as trouble transaction. Most people are mistaken when they believe that the hard part is getting a house into escrow. The most challenging part can be *keeping* the house in escrow, and *closing* escrow. Being a proactive leader in this process and effectively communicating with the listing agent, escrow/title, and the lender will help keep your escrow glued and close successfully.

SALES TIP: Facts tell, but stories sell. As you ride along with your mentor and experience more and more transactions of varying kind, you can use these experiences with your future clients as a way of easing concern, forewarning them of any potential red flags, or providing a solution to a sudden challenge during a transaction.

This hands-on experience gives you a foundation for reference when you are off on your own some day and may need a reference. Your mentor will also give you a fast track to operating your own real estate business. If what they are doing is working for their business, you can more easily apply their already successful model along as implement your own style of doing things.

While this book does outline a very easy to follow guide to success, it does leave room for much of your own style and personality to be applied. Being authentic and organic is so important in sales. Most people can spot a phony from a mile away.

Two

Choosing a Broker

Once you take and pass your state sales agent license exam, you will need to find a brokerage to partner with. In California, the state sales agent license requires you to partner with a brokerage in order to conduct real estate business. (Check your specific state requirements for a sales agent license vs. a broker license.) The brokerage is the big name that you will partner with in branding your new real estate business, ultimately pumping life into your future success. A few larger brokerages are Coldwell Banker, Alain Pinel, Better Homes and Gardens, Zephyr, and Sotheby's International. Choosing the right brokerage is as important as choosing the right healthcare- the details matter!

Here are the most important aspects to consider when deciding which broker is right for you:

- Commission split: New agents typically get anywhere between 50 to 65 percent of their overall earned commission from a transaction. The more business you produce, the higher your split becomes.

TIP: Every agent's commission split is negotiable. If you do choose to partner with a mentor, you can likely have your license administratively filed under your mentor's so you also get the commission split that the mentor has earned in your office; this relationship can benefit you since your mentor has likely produced enough business to be rewarded with a higher commission split than a beginner would get. The downside to the structure is that you have to then split your check with your mentor, depending on what you agree on.

- Location: While realtors are typically independent contractors and therefore can work from wherever they like, choosing a prime office is extremely important. You'll want to ask how much business the office does in addition to the overall market share of the brokerage. The larger the market share, the heavier the hitter in the eyes of potential sellers and buyers.

- Marketing materials: To me, this is *the* most important item to scrutinize with a fine eye. Take a look at the brochures, logo, stationary, website, color scheme, reputation within your community, ad campaigns, and even the For Sale signs of potential brokerages. These items will ultimately represent you in your business. Make sure the brokerage you choose has a high-quality marketing selection for their agents.

- Office fees: A couple thousand dollars a year for office fees is typical in the Bay Area at most brokerages. Additional fees typically apply if you want to reserve a designated desk space or cubicle. Some brokerages allow their agents to divide their office fees over their first four transactions. Just to forewarn you, office spaces are usually not terribly glamorous. Some brokerage can house over a hundred agents, so finding space and utilizing it in order to accommodate all those agents can be tough.

Cubicles are usually small, and multiple agents are assigned to each one. While this may not be the image of success you had originally imagined, I can assure you that being in the office as a new agent is really important.

TIP: Remember in Chapter 1 when we discussed the importance of having a mentor? Another bonus is that you can coattail on their paid-for office space rather than bum it at an uncomfortable "commuter desk," as we call them in the biz.

Getting Trained

One of the biggest challenges new agents face, other than that they have no clue where to even start, is that they can't yet answer any of the tough (or not-so-tough) questions that many buyers and sellers frequently ask. The state exam provides no in-the-field know-how, and this leaves many new agents lost in the dust once they leave the exam room with their passing ticket.

In order to be successful at anything, you must completely immerse yourself in as much information and experience as possible. Whichever brokerage you have decided to partner with will likely have a plethora of training materials and seminars for you to attend. Take every opportunity you can to learn and soak up your new trade.

It is important to know that people do ask the hard questions and you need to be able to know where to look for the answers. One tactic for handling this, especially in the beginning of your career before you have first hand experience to answer with, is the listen, write, pause, and research method. Listen to the buyer or seller's question or concern and write it down exactly. Tell them you will get back to them as soon as possible and want to do a little research before providing them with a concrete answer. Then actually do the research. Ask someone like managing broker, or research the web. Most frequently asked questions can easily be answered by reviewing the disclosure packet or simply by asking the listing agent.

Be sure to take full advantage of the resources available to you through the National Association of Realtors, as well as through your state and local boards. Your membership in the National Association of Realtors will likely be required by your brokerage, but you can absolutely get your money's worth by watching the countless webinars they have, attending any of their free and for-cost seminars, and reading their monthly newsletters. As in any profession, real estate laws and codes are constantly changing, and so are many other factors affect the housing market; keep your knowledge up-to-date.

Three

ESTABLISHING YOUR PERSONAL BRAND

Partnering with a solid brokerage is the first step in branding your new real estate business. However, in order to create a substantial and reputable presence as a local realtor and stand out against the other hundreds of agent your brokerage may also house, you will need to brand yourself as an individual, accordingly.

Social media presence and an online presence are essential to your success as a realtor. The "new" homebuyer, and more tech savvy homeowner are identifying best with a realtor that shares this ability to be technologically relevant. Not only will participating in social media, along with having a clean and useful website, generate and foster your leads, but these tools will also give you credibility when potential buyers and sellers are considering asking you to represent them.

The following are the social media outlets you definitely need to be present on:

- LinkedIn. LinkedIn is a website for professionals to interact and stay in touch with other professionals, both in their fields as well as in others. Some people use LinkedIn to look for employment opportunities and others use it has a way of substantiating their professional reputation.

- Zillow. Zillow is a very popular search resource for both buyers and sellers. Buyers are looking at available properties, and sellers are looking at their own potential home value. Having an agent profile on Zillow really puts you where the more typical buyer or seller is starting their preliminary thoughts of either buying or selling.

- Facebook. While many people have their personal beliefs on mixing business with personal life, Facebook does offer a way of making your business into a page, as well as offering paid advertising space for your services. Their advertising technology is very sophisticated and if used correctly, this may be a great avenue to generate leads for relatively little cost.

- Twitter. Twitter is used by the larger media sources, so being relevant on Twitter and learning the nuances of their system will really benefit your reputation and could lead to some great free of charge advertising.

- Pinterest. The new homebuyer is likely simultaneously searching for interior design ideas on websites, like Pinterest. Pinterest can be used to capture photos and attach a link to a blog post or article. This could be a useful way of directing traffic to your website.

- Instagram. Instagram is purely photo and hash tag based marketing. If used correctly and the nuances discovered, Instagram can be used to generate traffic to your website.

- If managing your social media presence is either too much effort or time, or just totally above your head in terms of tech savvy-ness, there are plenty of low cost options for hiring companies to manage your online social media profiles.

Below are a few links to social media management services to consider:

- www.sprinklr.com
- www.mercury360.com
- www.fanpilot.com
- www.netvibes.com

On top of your social media profiles, you will need to have a personalized and comprehensive personal website. While building a website can cost anywhere from $10 to a few hundred thousand dollars, you can build a very basic level site at a reasonable cost by finding a good hosting company that is easy to use and has a 24 hour tech hot line. My personal favorite is bluehost.com because it is so easy to use and they do have a customer service phone number.

Here are a few links to platforms for hosting and creating your website:

- www.godaddy.com
- www.wordpress.com
- www.wordpress.org
- www.bluehost.com

Four

Identifying Your Sphere of Influence

A great way to start getting your name out there is to let the people you know, know! Sit down with a pen and paper, and write down the name of every single person you know. Literally. When racking your brain for contacts, think of your college roommates, your high school friends, your mothers' club friends, your family, your wedding list, your neighbors, your parent's closest friends—everyone. This list that you just created is now your sphere of influence (SOI). It's estimated that an average of ten percent of your business will come from this list each year through your consistent follow up and interactions.

Once you have identified your sphere of influence and have compiled the appropriate mailing addresses and phone numbers, send a grand announcement that you are now a realtor!

TIP: If you really want to make a memorable splash on your sphere of influence, throw a "Welcome to Real Estate" party for yourself. Better yet, make it a block party and include all of your neighbors.

Stay in front of your sphere of influence on a monthly basis. You'd be surprised at how many cousins and old college friends forget you're a real estate expert when it comes time to sell or buy. Make them remember that you are a real estate professional and that they can trust you to be the best.

No matter whom you encounter daily, even if you have no property showings and are running around town in your yoga pants or jeans, tell everyone you know, talk to, or run into that you are the busiest realtor ever and this is your first downtime in over a week. (Fake that success until you make that success, baby!)

Here are some ideas of ways to stay in front of your sphere of influence:

- Send holiday cards or memorable small gifts, such as movie tickets.

- Provide market updates of recently sold homes similar to theirs in size and location, in areas that affect their home values.

- Host referral contests. For example, you might list of host of prizes and give a set of dates for people to send you referrals. Whoever sends you the most referrals that you end up closing gets a prize of the winner's choice.

- Pick up the phone—let people know what has sold in their neighborhoods this month.

- Throw a block party and host some snacks and beverages or a bounce house.

- Text or call personally at least 10 SOI contacts each month with a specialized monthly real estate market update for them.

- Donate to a charity in their name and send them the write-off—always a winner!

- Add your information to sports schedule magnets. They work.

- Send quarterly magnets and other branding doodads.

Identifying Your Farm Area

In real estate, a farm is simply a geographical area, or specific neighborhood that you regularly send mail to, door knock, and remind that you are their go-to realtor. Farming is used for personal branding and creating a household name that has proven to yield positive results over a longer period of time. It typically takes anywhere from one to five years to see lucrative results from consistently farming a neighborhood.

While most new agent's first hunch is to choose the neighborhood they grew up in (as was my original attempt at farming) or one that consists of high-value homes (my second trap of wasted postage), other factors may lead to a more successful farm.

The most important thing to consider when choosing which neighborhoods to farm is what the turnover rate is. How many homes usually sell each year in this neighborhood? If it's a sleepy neighborhood filled with long-term residents whom just finished paying off their homes, they probably have no plans of selling in the next five years, if ever in their lifetime.

TIP: Even if there is another self-proclaimed neighborhood expert in sight, don't let that discourage you. It's estimated that the top producer in any given geographical area still only gets 5 percent of the

local business. That leaves 95 percent for the rest of us. Go for the low-hanging fruit as a new agent. You'll get some of that 95 percent soon enough.

It is just as important to stay in front of your farm on a monthly basis as it is to stay in front of your sphere of influence. Even if you aren't receiving calls and e-mails from your farm just yet, every time people see your name and face on marketing materials— even while throwing it in the recycling bin—they are subconsciously connecting you with their neighborhood real estate.

Once you identify the areas you would like to farm, you will need to find a title company representative to work with that you can request a list of all houses that fit your desired home owner criteria and labels containing the homeowners' names. The title company that your brokerage works with, or any other that you develop a relationship with, has access to a plethora of data that will allow you to fine-tune your target client base. You can be as specific as requesting 300 homes in a specific area, that have not sold or transferred title within the last 3 years, 5 years, or even 20 years, depending on the intention of your mailer.

If your mailer is targeted towards a homeowner that may be growing out of their home due to family expansion, you would want to target those who have owned their home for something like 3 to 5 years. If your mailer is targeting a homeowner that maybe wanting to downsize their digs, you would send your mailers to those homes that have not transferred title or sold in over 15 to 20 years.

The title company representative that you have chosen to work with will be more than happy to provide you with free labels and farm lists in hope that when you do get something into escrow, you'll open escrow with them. This relationship with a title company representative may be the most invaluable you will make.

The title company rep will want to help you market your business so that when you do find a client and get something into escrow, that you open escrow with them. Escrow and Title Company are one and the same. Most of the larger brokerages partner with one and tend to use them the most, but you can make your own connections with other companies.

Here are some ideas of ways to stay in front of your farm:

- Send monthly market updates on what's newly active on the market, what's pending, and what has just sold in their specific neighborhood. This information keeps potential sellers excited about their own home values. No matter what their plans for the future, there is usually a certain number that will make most people sell.

- Invest in sports schedule magnets; they actually work. Your pretty or handsome face, name, and contact information will be on hundreds of refrigerators, at least for one sports season. I *am* a realtor, and obviously my parents would never even dream of using or recommending any other realtor to their network of friends, but their neighborhood realtor sends these each season, and his face hangs out on their fridge all year long. Genius.

- Write and send a relevant community newsletter to the homeowners in your farm. Include local eatery deals, upcoming estate or garage sales, charity and volunteer opportunities, seasonal articles, and general safety tips. After creating a track record of relevant information for your readers, this will no doubt win some readership.

- Host referral contests—see Chapter 5 for more information on these.

Five

Marketing with Mailers

and Door Knocking

Any veteran real estate agent will tell you that the cheapest and best forms of marketing you can do for yourself are mailers and door knocking. Using your God given extremities to move and shake- what a concept!

Marketing with Mailers

The types of mailers you can send to your farm, sphere of influence, and any other random neighborhood you get from your title company rep can range from direct-mail marketing campaigns sent through a third-party vendor to personal handwritten notes. Your brokerage likely has pre-branded campaigns you can choose from, and usually your annual office fee covers a percentage of the cost.

Here are a few mailer ideas:

- Buyers soliciting an off-market opportunity—this is a *great* opportunity to double-end a listing, which means to represent both buyer and seller in the transaction. You would address the letter specifically to the homeowner by name and give a summary about your prospective buyers. Explain that while your clients have been writing and submitting competitive offers, they are missing out by just a few thousand dollars. They are looking for something off market and are prepared to make a competitive offer if their home should be the right fit. This mailer has personally been the most successful and inexpensive way I have obtained listings and listing leads.

MARKETING TIP: The best part about this form of inexpensive marketing is that while you should certainly be able to produce a buyer, you don't necessarily have to have one waiting in the wings when you send the mailer. You can use this has a foot in the door to a great listing opportunity. Buyers are

plentiful in most markets so don't wait for the buyer find the perfect off market opportunity first!

- Interest-rate change forecasts—"Now is the time to sell." This reminds potential sellers that without qualified and ready buyers, home values won't continue to rise as they have been. If interest rates increase, many would-be investors, and first time homebuyers alike, will drop out of the housing market, making their home less competed for.

- Expired listings—check your local MLS weekly for listings that have just expired. Mail a personalized letter to the sellers, and ask for an opportunity to show them how you can sell their homes this time around.

- For-sale-by-owners (FSBO)—check Craigslist and your local paper for owners who think they can sell their homes better than a professional can. The key to these people is realizing that you're likely dealing with know-it-alls. Play up your assets and show that with professional marketing, you can sell their homes for a higher price and with added legal protection.

- Referral Contests. Entice your sphere and farm to refer any one thinking about buying or selling in the near future to you. Create a set of parameters and think of some cool prizes that would appeal to your target reader.

TIP: One seminar I attended stressed the two key factors to successful selling were fear and greed. Appealing to these two natural human instincts will help corral your potential lead to convert to an actual client.

Door Knocking

Door knocking is best done with a purpose and a leave-behind item such as a neighborhood market update on what's recently sold and how their values may be affected. The goal of a door knock is to get people's contact information so you can stay in front of them every ninety days. (Notice a theme?)

TIP: In order to avoid looking like you're peddling religion or vacuum cleaners, I advise that you don't wear all black while door knocking. Opt for something more inviting and welcoming. Remember that a genuine smile is always your best outfit choice. The most effective door knocking takes place between 2:00 p.m. and 5:00 p.m. on weekdays or anytime on Saturdays. Set a goal for ten houses a day until you have knocked on every home in your farm. Then it's time for round two.

Here are a few more door knocking leave-behind ideas to help charm your farm and set you apart from your real estate peddling competition:

- New Year's Day or Valentine's Day—sparkling apple cider with your card attached to the ribbon.
- Fall or beginning of winter—fire-starting log with your card attached.
- Fourth of July—American flag with your card attached.
- Halloween—safety tips and miniature pumpkins with your card attached.

Six

Holding Open Houses

One of the questions I am asked most frequently is "Does your company give you leads to work on?" The answer, my friends, is a big, fat "Heck, no." You'll have to find business on your own in this business. Before you panic and let your bubble burst, remember that I have written this handbook to help you with just that- finding business!

In addition to consistently sending mailers to your sphere of influence, your farm, and various other neighborhoods that pique yours—or one of your buyers'—interest along the way, both new and veteran realtors do open houses to get listing and buyer leads.

When buyers come to preview the home, if they are not already working with a realtor, you can take down their information in hopes of helping them find their new home and representing them in that transaction.

Alternatively, if a neighbor comes in to see how his or her home may compare because he or she is thinking of selling it, you can take his or her information in hopes of setting a home valuation meeting. You can then follow up with them every 90 days or so to remind them that when they do consider selling, you are their go-to agent and have developed a relationship with them along the wait.

To find an open house to hold, simply e-mail or call agents directly on new properties in the MLS. You can also ask your office's marketing coordinator to send an e-mail blast or make a meeting announcement for you.

TIP: To leave a lasting impression on both potential buyers and potential listing leads, offer champagne and muffins—or wine and cheese or juice and cookies—at your open house.

TIP: It's also a good idea to door knock the street at least two hours before your open house to personally invite the neighbors to the open house. Your listing leads will come from these neighbors.

Paying for Leads

Ever heard the old saying that "it takes money to make money"? It doesn't always have to be true, but it does help. Success usually takes a winning combination of time and hard work, but you can certainly speed up the process by deciding to purchase a lead-generating service.

Lead-generating services range in cost from a percentage of your overall commission of a closed sale, to a fixed monthly figure for a certain number of guaranteed leads. Monthly fees for these services range from fifty dollars to upward of two thousand dollars a month. Before you pay, ask where and how these leads are generated. For example, on my personal real estate website, www.shopsanfranciscohomes.com, users can click so many times before being asked to enter in their contact information. I then get notified of a lead searching and have access to their search history and searching trends. This is just one example of a lead generating option.

Another paid lead generating option is to hire a third party service that analyzes a particular geographical area, then sends them tailored post cards with a special entry code associated with it. This entices recipients to head to the mentioned website, enter their code, and be able to receive an estimate of their current home value. You would receive a notification of this potential seller lead, and be able to reach out to them by their address and any other information that they provided on the home value site. The paid-for-lead options are pretty endless depending on your budget.

Here are a few links to lead-generating services to check out that I have personally used to drum up business:

- www.Zurple.com
- www.Zillow.com
- www.TigerLead.com
- www.SmartZip.com

Networking

No matter how much business you purchase or how many mailers you send, nothing beats creating personal connections and fostering organic relationships. Try joining a club or becoming more involved in your community through volunteering or through your children's schools and after school clubs. No matter where you go, make sure you are friendly and gracious and always mention that you are a realtor. As you build trust within these circles, you will build a referral base as well.

If you want people to regard you as their trustworthy, go-to community expert, you have to act the part. Be the community expert. Learn everything you can about your community and the area in which you plan to practice your business. Here are a few ways to get involved in your community:

- Join a country club.
- Sponsor your local sports teams.
- Contribute to a local charity.
- Volunteer regularly with local organizations like Habitat for Humanity.
- Throw a block party.
- Get involved in bettering your local schools.
- Join your local mothers' club.
- Attend your local church and become involved in the parish or congregation.
- Connect with your local construction contractors to get a leg up on local home improvement trends.
- If you have children, use them. Everyone loves a cute kid. And children have friends with parents—cha-ching!

Seven

Determining Market Value

Knowing how to price a piece of property is your single biggest value as a realtor. You must have a pulse on your local real estate market. If your pricing is off, your buyers don't get their offers accepted. If your pricing is off, you don't close a sale on that amazing listing that your mailers or consistent door knocking snagged you.

Here is a full proof strategy for gaining general knowledge of your local real estate market:
1. Look in your local Multiple Listing Service, or MLS, (a database that has every single on-market home for sale, a as well as all previously sold homes) for recently sold properties. It really depends on your local market, but

in today's San Francisco Bay Area real estate market, I typically don't have to go back more than 90 to 120 days to get a good idea of the prices properties have been selling for in that specific area. Calculate the cost per square footage on the sold properties so that you can more easily compute a somewhat accurate calculation of sales price when first showing a property to a buyer, or first meeting with your potential seller.

TIP: You must look at homes with similar features. Think "apples, to apples". Match bedroom count to bedroom count and bathroom count to bathroom count. Square footage should be roughly the same, but in some areas it may be hard to get an exact match.

2. If you're doing a comparable analysis for a listing appointment, call the listing agents of recently sold properties to ask how many offers they have received and how many disclosures were downloaded. This will give a good indication of buyer traffic in that neighborhood. High demand creates competition among buyers.

TIP: Competition among buyers then creates a bidding war, which ultimately results in selling for a higher price.

3. If you're representing a buyer in a transaction, find out how many disclosures have been downloaded by asking the listing agent. As mentioned above, this gives you an idea of the interest in the property. In the Bay Area, it is pretty typical that for every offer received, two disclosures have been downloaded. So if ten disclosures have been downloaded, you should expect around five offers to be submitted.

TIP: Your offer should reflect the demand.

4. Take the condition of the property into consideration. If the home needs a new foundation, new plumbing, and a new roof, those items should be accounted for in price and comparable analyses. Alternatively, if a property was just recently upgraded or remodeled, you should consider that as well.

5. If you are representing the buyers in a transaction, it is important to know what the property is worth to your buyers. If your buyers have fallen in love, the home will certainly be worth more than the asking price, and the price they believe their competition is coming in at. If you are representing the sellers,

their idea of their home value could be different than you believe due to emotional attachment.

TIP: Don't focus on the percentage over the asking price homes may be selling for. Focus on the above items to determine where you should advise your buyers to begin bidding. Remember that ultimately the market determines the sales price.

Eight

WORKING WITH BUYERS, WRITING OFFERS, AND ANSWERING BUYER QUESTIONS

Working with Buyers

Today's buyers expect instant answers and prompt attention, leaving an agent something like eight to ten minutes to respond to a lead before the buyer has moved on to another agent for information. Let me stress the importance of immediate follow-up. I cannot tell you how many lost opportunities occur because agents don't get in contact with the prospective lead right away.

TIP: The biggest and best buyer advice I can give you is to PICK UP THE PHONE. Calling a prospect

is one thousand times more likely to yield a client conversion than just emailing them. Phone skills are learned through practice. Prepare yourself mentally for hundreds of awkward conversations before you start to get your groove going, but trust me- you will get the hang of it!

While it is important to promptly follow up with a potential buyer lead, it is also just as important to weed out the hot leads from the cold leads.

In today's real estate market, most buyers begin their home searches anywhere from six months to a year before they are ready to buy. It is important identify the buyers who are six months to a year away from actually making a home investment so you can focus your time on the buyers who are serious and ready to invest when they find the right property.

A buyer who is worth your time and can be considered your *ideal* buyer will meet these three qualifications:

1. The buyer is not already working with a real-tor. It is important and totally appropriate to ask this up front in your initial contact.

2. The buyer is preapproved or willing to get preapproved immediately with a lender you recommend. Don't expend effort showing

properties to buyers before they are preapproved. Too many buyers have unrealistic ideas of what they can actually afford. It's called the "champagne taste with a beer wallet" syndrome.

3. The buyer is willing to meet you at your office or for coffee to discuss home search criteria and meet you in person. If buyers aren't willing to do that, they are likely not ready to purchase, and you shouldn't waste too much of your time or energy pursuing them.

    Remain confident that there are qualified buyers out there by the plenty, but also know that in your pursuit of this ideal client, you will come across plenty of not-so-ideal buyers. Many buyers either have an unrealistic idea of what they can afford, of what is actually available, or they are just plain looking with no intention of buying. This individual simply enjoys attending open houses and soaking up the free cookies and juice.

    Every couple of months you'll hear about a fake buyer that either tried to rope agents into driving them around for hours and hours with no intention of buying, or something more illegal such as having an agent submit an offer on their behalf in some sort of money fraud scheme. This has actually happened to me personally very early on in my career.

I was helping a buyer lead that came in off one of our company's widely used Internet lead systems. This buyer said they were overseas working on an oilrig and would be coming to San Francisco at the end of July with his wife and needed to purchase a small condo before. He said he was an all cash buyer. While many of you are already thinking this sounds like a scam, I can assure you that in a city like San Francisco, this scenario is very common and sales do happen with them.

I sent him many properties to view on-line, and he found options on his own as well. We communicated for weeks via email. He said he was unable to speak on the phone initially because he was on the oilrig, and he conveniently missed each of our scheduled phone appointments. Again, I know what you are thinking. Since he said he was an all cash buyer, I requested his proof of funds and he actually did provide three statements. He also used the real estate attorney that I send many of my clients to in order to aid him in the transaction and keep his deposit money in trust so that we could proceed when we get into contract on a property.

We proceeded to email back and forth, answering his normal buyer questions and sending disclosures and video tours of properties. I even wrote three offers for him, one of which would have been accepted but the listing agent was not comfortable with the proof of funds that I submitted. Almost instantly after getting request for more information on the funds, I get a call from the attorney saying my buyers deposit check bounced. Yes readers, *this* was where I realized we had been wrapped up in a fake buyer scam.

Answering Buyer Questions

Now that you've determined what makes buyers qualified to work with you, you are ready to show them properties and address all of their questions.

Here are the questions I am asked most frequently:

How much of a down payment do I need?

A down payment of 20 percent is the minimum in order to be competitive in most areas. Depending on your local market, some down payment assistance programs may be available.

I like this house; how do I know if it is a good investment?

Be aware of local home values and their historic trends. But in general, when examining a home with your buyer, assess the plumbing, foundation, roof, windows, and heating and electrical systems.

What do homeowner's association fees cover, and what is a typical fee?

A homeowner's association (HOA) is a collection of all the owners in a building or complex. All owners are assessed fees to cover maintenance of the grounds and building; sometimes HOA fees also include insurance, electricity, water, and garbage. There is no typical fee. Fees can range from $50 per month all the way to $2,500 per month.

Why should I get preapproved? I already know how much I want to spend.

Getting preapproved before seeing any properties is important for three reasons. First, while your buyers may have an idea of what they are comfortable spending on a mortgage each month, the final monthly cost can change drastically depending on what loan type they qualify for. Second, properties may move quickly when inventory levels are low. If buyers are serious about finding the right homes, they will need to have their preapproval ready to go when submitting offers. Finally, while many people believe they know what they can realistically afford each month, lenders may view their financial situations differently. While most people do like to window-shop, no one likes the disappointment of not being able even to submit an offer on a home they have fallen in love with. I can tell you that this happens all the time.

I want to avoid a bidding war. What can I do?

Identify the specific neighborhoods that your clients are looking in. Write a letter to all homes in that area that meet their search criteria, identifying what your clients want and their willingness to put together a competitive offer if the property is the right fit. You can obtain a list of these qualifying homes through your title company representative.

Helping Your Clients Make an Offer

Yay! You have successfully found your buyers a home that they would like to submit an offer on. Keep in mind that all states, cities, and offices have different requirements for this; however, this generalized time line and to-do list may help:

1. Request all of the disclosures from the listing agent. Ask how many disclosure packages have been given out. A disclosure package is a compilation of all reports, and documents that have to do with the property.

2. Contact your buyer's lender and fill the lender in on the property type and offer price. Make sure that the buyer's loan approval will apply to this specific property based on its quality and condition. At this point, you'll need the lender to send you a preapproval letter specific to the property. An example of this would be if you were submitting an offer on a condo, but that condo happens to be over a laundry mat. Some lenders will not lend on this. Another example would be purchasing a house that has a broken window, or

dry rotted staircase. Some lenders won't lend on a property with these conditions.

3. Have your clients review and sign all disclosures and offer documents. It is so important that before they invest, they really understand what condition the property is in, the known history of the property, and know about any foreseeable needed future repairs.

4. Check with the listing agent for any special requirements or terms that the sellers would like to see included in your offer. You'll want to make your offer as competitive as possible, and that means adhering to the seller's requests 100 percent. An example of a special seller request would be a free rent-back, where they are allowed to remain in the home for a set period of time after the close of escrow free of charge.

5. Write your offer. Ask your mentor or managing broker to help you with the first few. Your offer needs to be clean, complete, and fully signed.

6. Submit your offer, signed disclosures, and copies of your client's deposit check and pre-approval letter to the listing agent as directed. Cross your fingers!

Nine

There are endless approaches to a successful listing appointment. All realtors have their own professional style, and as long as you get a listing agreement signed and the house sold for the highest price possible, any approach can be considered successful.

Although you will develop your own professional style, you may find that these tips, combined with an organic knowledge and understanding of your local real estate market, and the home buying and selling process, will lead to a successful listing appointment:

- Reserve all pricing judgments until after seeing the property in person. Anything can sound perfect and high-end on paper. In order to properly analyze comparable properties for pricing determination, you must see the condition of the property in person.

- Research as much as you can about the property and the area.

- Make sure your clothes look clean and professional. First impressions are everything, and people generally do judge a book by its cover.

- Take notes. When you are taking your initial look at the property, ask if it is OK to take notes as you tour. This shows that you are very detail oriented and that you will properly analyze their property.

- Let them talk. You'll be amazed at how successful your close ratio will be if you just shut up and let the potential sellers do the talking.

- Showcase your marketing strategies. Bring sample brochures, marketing materials, and a list of the popular websites your client's home will be featured on. Tell clients about your "amazingly successful" open houses and how you put your unique touch on every detail. (Feel free to tailor this as you see fit; you know your strengths better than I do.)

- Get the listing agreement signed before you leave the first appointment, and head to your office to turn the freshly signed listing documents in. It's time to work!

- Request a second meeting before you leave the first one to present your finalized pricing analysis of what the home will likely sell for.

- Although there are many strategies to this part of the listing appointment, I urge you to be as honest and straightforward about this as you can be. Some agents feel it works best to inflate the selling price in hopes of falsely promising the right number in terms of expected sales price. This strategy is very risky. If you promise and don't deliver, you're definitely not likely to close the transaction or get any future referrals.

- Send a personalized thank-you note immediately.

Ten

Summarizing Success

Consistency is the key to being successful at anything, especially when you have the right tools and road map. I've personally attended many seminars that promise to teach you every sales trick in the book. In my personal experience, the best "trick" anyone can use is repetition. Keep mailing, keep door knocking, and keep doing open houses because eventually your success gate will open, and transactions will start to pour in.

Being a realtor comes with great highs and can also come with some very low lows. If at any point in the beginning of your career you feel as though you'll never find a client, never get an offer accepted, or never get a paycheck, remind yourself that like anything built soundly, the foundation of your career is being set, and soon enough success will follow. Follow the road map that I have outlined for you in this book, and repeat, repeat, repeat.

Lastly, I'll remind you that it is important to always plan for tomorrow and never stop feeding your pipeline. Even if you have four homes in escrow, you need to keep searching for the next four. If you don't have any buyers or sellers in your immediate pipeline, you don't have a paycheck in your pipeline.

I wish you the very best success in your new real estate career.

A special thank you to my real estate mentor, Anthony Navarro. Anthony Navarro is currently a top real estate producer with Coldwell Banker based in San Francisco. You can find more information on Anthony on his website, http://www. NavarroRE.com.